Jane Brocket's CLEVER CONCEPTS

Ruby, Violet, Lime

Looking for COLOR

Millbrook Press · Minneapolis

We live in a world full of
COLOR.

Let's look around to see
what colors we can find.

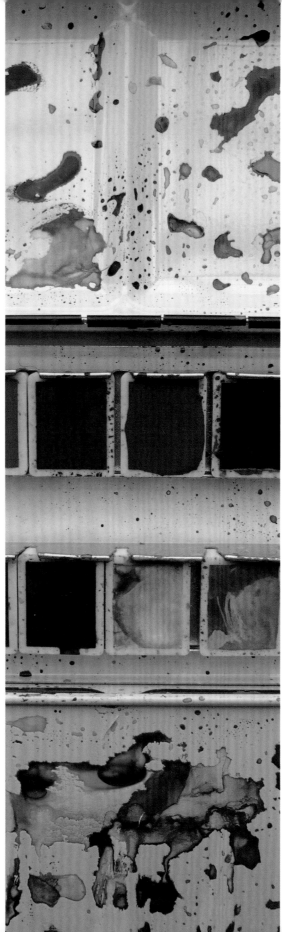

3

There are three primary colors.
Red. yellow. Blue.

Primary colors are pure colors.
They can't be made by mixing
different colors together.

Red is bright and bold.
Scarlet candy, ruby flowers,
crimson chairs, and rosy
apples say, "Look at me!"

yellow is light and sunny.

A primrose cupcake, lemon tiles, a butter-yellow door, and a vase of golden daffodils are cheerful and welcoming.

Blue is a peaceful color. It is also easy to find. Turquoise pools, navy boots, aqua sneakers, and indigo jeans are cool and calm.

11

We can mix primary colors to make more colors.

Yellow and **blue** make **green**.

Red and **yellow** make **orange**.

Blue and **red** make **purple**.

Green, **orange**, and **purple** are secondary colors.

Green is crisp and lively. Lime frosting, mint-green striped socks, emerald lettuces, and jade gardens are fresh and zingy.

Orange is hot and fiery. Copper berries, a tangerine sunset, amber peppers, and flame-colored flowers make every season feel warm.

Purple can be tricky to find. But look carefully. You might discover mauve frosting, violet flowers, plum eggplants, and a lavender shed. What other colors can we find?

Brown is warm and earthy. We can find it in lots of everyday things: tan cookies, tawny bricks, a terra-cotta plant pot, and chestnut cubes of fudge.

22

Pink can be pale or bright. Blush-pink blossoms and salmon ribbons are sweet. Bubblegum buildings, magenta shoes, and hot pink flowers are shocking.

23

Don't forget **black** and white!

Black is strong and serious. Jet-black staircases, coal-colored bricks, and ebony iron gates will last for years.

White is pure and clean.
Pearl-white snow and ivory
flowers are beautiful, but
they don't last very long.

When black and white
are mixed together, they
make gray. Can you find
something gray here?

Silver and **gold** are metallic colors. They make things look special. Sprinkles on a cupcake, spray paint, a door knocker, and a skyscraper all sparkle and shine.

Every color we have found comes in many shades. Some are pale and pastel, like a peachy dog and soft pink and primrose yellow buildings.

Others are dark and deep like glowing stained glass windows; the shadowy night sky; and inky, stripy socks.

We have found lots of
COLOR!

Do you have a favorite?
Or do you like them all?

Text and photographs copyright © 2012 by Jane Brocket

Millbrook Press
A division of Lerner Publishing Group, Inc.
241 First Avenue North
Minneapolis, MN 55401 U.S.A.

Website address: www.lernerbooks.com

Additional images in this book are used with the permission of:
© Phoebe Brocket, pp. 17 (sunset) and 29 (night sky); © iStockphoto.com/elaine (cardboard background); © iStockphoto.com/Winston Davidian (textured paper background).

Main body text set in Chaloops Regular 24/32.
Typeface provided by Chank.

Library of Congress Cataloging-in-Publication Data

Brocket, Jane.
    Ruby, violet, lime : looking for color / text and photographs by Jane Brocket.
        p.   cm. — (Jane Brocket's clever concepts)
    ISBN 978-0-7613-4612-8 (lib. bdg. : alk. paper)
    1. Colors—Juvenile literature. I. Title.
 QC495.5.B75 2012
 535.6—dc22   2010051757

Manufactured in the United States of America
1 — MG — 7/15/11

For Ellie and Amy
—J.B.

With many thanks to Carol Hinz, Mary Rodgers, and Danielle Carnito